Australia Here We Come!

Exploring a distant place

**Wendy North and
Ann Hamblen**

Geography Plus: Primary Teachers' Toolkit

Series Editors: **Paula Owens and Paula Richardson**

Geographical
Association

Editors' preface

Geography matters. It is part and parcel of our personal survival kit, helping us to know not just where places are, but what they are like, why and how they are changing, and how we feel about them. Geography enables us to identify and explain relationships between people, places and environments and to understand connections between our everyday lives and the wider world. In a world that is often messy and unpredictable, geography helps us to make sense of who we are and how we fit in.

Children today are growing up in an increasingly globalised world. The workplace of tomorrow is likely to have stronger international dimensions while the jobs of tomorrow may not yet have been invented. Children will benefit from an education that enables them to understand how the world works, to make sense of world events and to critique an increasing array of information in doing so. Geography contributes to this. It is a fundamental requirement of a 21st-century education.

Geography, as a subject, is a valuable curriculum resource. All of the titles in this series draw on enduring elements of geography knowledge and skills, using a geographical lens to focus enquiry about the real world while making relevant links with other subjects. We have taken an 'adopt, adapt and innovate' approach by providing lesson resources which offer you the scope for active 'curriculum making', allowing you to work with and interpret the national curriculum to your best advantage. We hope that you will add in your own knowledge and skills and your pupils' experiences to create engaging and challenging lessons that work for you and your class.

The titles in this series have been chosen to represent the extraordinary diversity of the world we live in and to allow teachers to achieve a good balance of geography through the choice of content. Each book includes aspects of the chosen topic which are interesting, informative and which have the ability to get children to enquire and debate. We believe that teachers are the key to high-quality, challenging and enjoyable learning experiences and hope that you find this book useful as you create your own curriculum.

Paula Owens and Paula Richardson, December 2010

Authors

Wendy North is a Geography Curriculum Consultant and former Primary Curriculum Development Consultant with the Geographical Association.

Ann Hamblen is a creative writer in schools.

Contents

Quick guide to lesson resources

Lesson 1: Let's fly to Australia
PowerPoint 1
Photoset 1
Knowledge box 2
World map

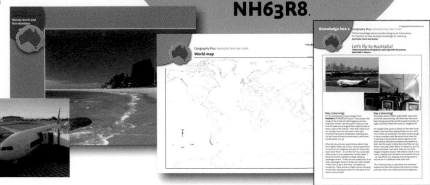

Lesson 2: What should we do in Sydney?
Activity sheets
  1: If I was in the picture
  2: What Jack and Charlotte did
  3: This is what they saw
PowerPoint 2
Knowledge box 3
Australia map

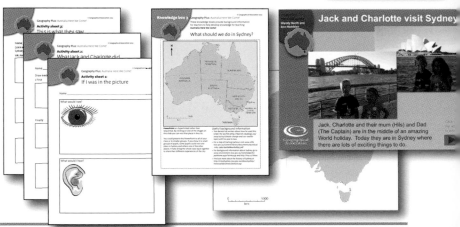

Lesson 3: What is it like to live in Australia?
Activity sheets
  4: Who am I?
  5: What can people do here?
  6: A good or not so good place?
PowerPoint 3
Photoset 2
Knowledge box 4
Australia map

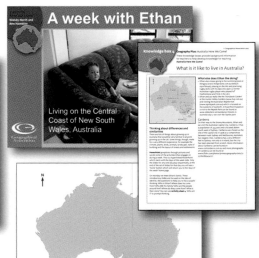

Lesson 4: The sun has got his hat on
Activity sheet
  7: What should Ethan take to the Snowy Mountains?
PowerPoints 3 and 4
Knowledge box 5
Australia map

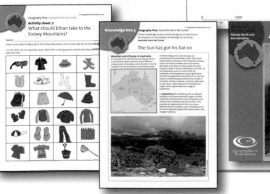

Lesson 5: Surfing the waves
Photoset 3
Knowledge box 6

Lesson 6: Experiencing Uluru
Activity sheet
 (Choose from pdf and
 PowerPoint versions)
 8: To climb or not to climb?
PowerPoint 5
Knowledge box 7
Australia map

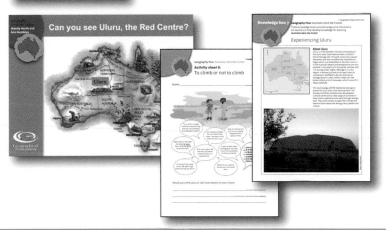

Lesson 7: Coral reef or rainforest?
PowerPoints 1 and 6
Photoset 4
Knowledge box 8
Australia map

Lesson 8: Sharing what we have learnt
Refer back to previous work done

Extras
Useful information:
 weblinks and references
Medium term plan
Knowledge box
 1: The geography of Australia
Glossary

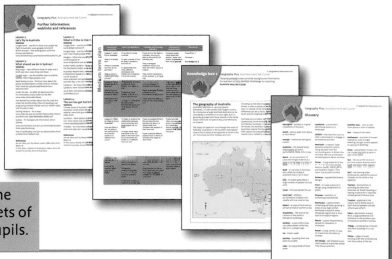

Make sure you look at the 'Notes' on the PowerPoints which offer useful snippets of information and questions for your pupils.

Why teach about Australia?

Developing understanding of the wider world

A distant place

To learn more about places and the way that people live in the them has always been a key objective of primary geography. The familiarity of films such as *Finding Nemo* and picture books such as *Window* (Baker, 1991) and *Where the Forest Meets the Sea* (Baker, 1989) makes Australia a place that young pupils and their teachers may already have experienced second-hand or, in some cases, know quite well.

A study of Australia provides pupils with an opportunity to think about some easily recognisable things they have in common with children who live on the other side of the globe, e.g. food, education and leisure,

before we ask them to think about the lives of people in other places that may appear to be very different.

Diversity

Australia, by the nature of its size, also has an enormous range of differences for young pupils to explore. The vastness of the landscape, the variety of the climate and the magnificence of the wildlife make Australia worth investigating for these reasons alone.

Pupils' immediate fascination with aboriginal painting and story also allows us to explore a culture that is rooted in different experience, traditions and values. Engaging with native Australian culture enables us to celebrate and understand difference too, and to think about alternative ways to value and care for our world.

Connections with people and places

One of geography's key roles is to help pupils understand that we have many connections to people and places around the world, whether this is through travel, the food we eat or the clothes we wear. For many of us these connections are with family living elsewhere in the world and, because of our shared colonial heritage, many people in the UK have relatives in Australia, even if they are distant ones.

What connects us, the authors, most meaningfully to Australia in the times in between visits is the ability to use the internet, both email and Skype, to talk with family who live there. What is exciting about bringing geography alive in the age of the internet is the possibility of you in your school making similar connections with an Australian school – something that was unthinkable just a few years ago.

Why story matters

Narrative links are what help us to make sense of our learning and of our lives; without them everything is random and disconnected. While putting this book together, we held firmly to the idea of 'story' in its widest sense. We have included many stories: the true stories of Jack and Charlotte visiting Sydney and of Ethan's daily life on the Central Coast, New South Wales; the ancestral tales passed on by word-of-mouth by Australia's indigenous people for thousands of years; and some beautiful picture story-books.

This book itself provides the framework for a story – the story of a learning journey which each pupil will experience as you guide them through the activities.

References
Baker, J. (1989) *Where the Forest Meets the Sea*. London: Walker.
Baker, J. (1991) *Window*. London: Walker.

Prior and future learning

The book is aimed at years 1, 2 and 3 but can be adapted for use with other age groups.

Prior learning

During the Early Years Foundation Stage (EYFS) pupils are introduced to the wider world through the use of globes, images (including video), story-books and artefacts and share what they know through the drawing of simple maps, role-play, language and creative expression.

Pupils will have had some experience of looking at places in this kind of exploratory way, through the repeated cycle of first-hand, local investigation combined with global enquiries, the latter often through stories, festivals, artefacts and 'virtual' encounters.

Pupils who have explored their own outdoor environment and begun to develop the vocabulary to talk about their own place in the world will be in a position to talk about comparable situations in distant places and to express their views about the lives of the people who live there. They will be supported to do this through the use of resources and careful scaffolding of their learning. They will have the opportunity to think about their everyday lives, recognising some of the basic things that we all need, such as love and the care of our families, shelter, warmth, food and water. Feeling good about oneself and one's own locality is a prerequisite for a positive response to the lives of others who may, on the surface at least, live very different lives from our own.

Future learning

Throughout key stage 2 pupils should continue to build their knowledge of the wider world and of different societies and cultures, deepening their existing experience and developing their understanding of the relationship between places and the way people live their lives. By doing this they will begin to recognise how our lives are connected to other people and places, and how places fit within a wider geographical context.

Pupils need to learn that the life of people in one locality is not representative of the lives of all people in that country. Starting to explore this idea in the context of their own local area will build and support pupils' understanding when they learn about distant places.

During key stage 2 pupils will extend their understanding of environmental issues in a global context, learning about the ways people can improve and damage the environment and beginning to understand that their own choices can have global, as well as local, effects.

How to teach about Australia

Tailoring learning

This book and accompanying resources provide possible learning journeys for Foundation Stage pupils as well as for key stage 1 and younger key stage 2 pupils. Pupils reach such varied levels of development, and have such different learning needs through these years, that teachers become adept at adapting materials and activities, and personalising learning experiences. The ideas in this book might be shared in many different ways: in short 50-minute lessons, in longer, cross-curricular lessons, on several afternoons in a half term, or by a number of teachers who are looking for inspiration for a 'World Week'.

Adopt and adapt

The aim is that all pupils should reach the end of their study having experienced both the richness and variety of the vastness that is Australia, and also with more detailed understanding of at least one 'similar' and one 'different' place, keeping a balance of breadth and

depth. Within this, please choose and adapt content, structure (including the time you devote to the different learning opportunities in any given lesson) and activities confidently in the light of your pupils' learning needs and your learning objectives.

Using the minimum number of lessons, this basic balance could be achieved by choosing:
- the 'big picture' activity to gain a sense of the diversity of the Australian landscape
- a focus on one locality in greater depth; either Sydney, looked at through the eyes of children who are tourists, or the Central Coast, New South Wales, looked at through the eyes of an Australian child who lives there
- at least one of the lessons on Uluru, the Great Barrier Reef or

the Daintree Rainforest. You might then check to see whether you need to adapt some activities from other lessons to ensure suitable experiences in important areas, such as map use/map-making, to suit your pupils' needs.

Make the pupils go 'Wow!'

The most important factor in making *Australia Here We Come!* a success for pupils is the enthusiasm of their teacher. This book communicates the authors' passion and enthusiasm for, and love of, Australia: you in turn can generate great enthusiasm for enquiring about Australia.

Start with a story

All of the lessons are based on story, using a wide variety of different kinds of narrative as stimuli (see page 6). Story is a powerful way of communicating complex geographical knowledge and awareness to pupils, because narrative puts flesh and clothes on abstractions and generalisations, bringing them alive in our hearts and minds. If, through story and artwork, pupils have imaginatively experienced the Daintree Rainforest, and are emotionally engaged with the boy in *Where the Forest Meets the Sea* (Baker, 1989) and the possibility of modern development engulfing this ancient and amazing place, they are on the way to asking what they can or should do about such dilemmas in the future. Without imaginative involvement, leading to empathy, why should they care?

Keep a travel journal

The main tool, used in different ways throughout the sessions, is the travel journal (explained in **Knowledge box 1**). Frequent, short plenary sessions where pupils can discuss what they would like to put in their journals, or share what they have added, will keep the elements of this 'learning story' coherent and focussed for your pupils and contribute to an on-going dialogue about what they will include in the final sharing event (see Lesson 8). The pupils' travel journals will provide you with a way to talk about 'How we know we are better geography explorers now then when we started our work on Australia'.

Build in assessment for learning

Your pupils should review what they have learned and select from it in order to share it with others. Adding short plenaries throughout the unit will give different groups of pupils the chance to share and consolidate learning as well as provide assessment opportunities.

Assessment is an integral part of planning. We need to keep in mind from the outset the learning goals we have for our pupils and how we will know that they have achieved them, or that they need help to do so. See the assessment and progression diagram on page 33 for further details.

Key learning outcomes

Most pupils will be able to:
- use appropriate geographical vocabulary to talk about and describe some of the human and physical features of Australia
- express their views about different places and environments
- select information to help them answer questions
- use maps and globes to locate Australia and some of the locations studied
- draw simple maps to convey information
- make connections between their life in the UK and life in Australia.

Some pupils will not have made as much progress but will be able to:
- begin to use appropriate geographical vocabulary to

recognise some of the human and physical features of Australia
- talk about some of the features of everyday life in Australia
- say in simple terms what they like and don't like
- use resources with support to help answer questions
- use globes and large-scale maps to locate Australia and at least two major features
- begin to make connections between their life in the UK and life in Australia.

Some pupils will have progressed further and will be able to:
- use appropriate geographical vocabulary to begin to explain some of the human and physical features of Australia
- describe and compare some of the similarities and differences between places in Australia, and between everyday lives there and in the UK
- recognise how people try to sustain and improve environments
- give their views about Australia and begin to offer reasons
- begin to select resources and use them to seek and convey information
- make and use maps to show different kinds of information about Australia.

Summary

This book and accompanying resources offer pupils the

opportunity to explore some of the diversity of Australia through a series of lessons which are underpinned by story and the experiences of other children. They offer teachers the flexibility to select and adopt what they feel best suits their learners' needs and take pupils on a creative learning journey as they explore the complex country that is Australia.

Reference

Baker, J. (1989) *Where the Forest Meets the Sea*. London: Walker.

Ask yourself, am I building:
- an enthusiasm for finding out about the world?
- an awareness and knowledge of the world?
- an awareness that there are different ways to live in the world?
- an understanding that there are different landscapes and environments in the world?
- a realisation that there are different ways of representing the world spatially?
- a developing capacity to represent the world in simple maps?
- an awareness that, for example, writers, artists, native peoples, geographers and children (not mutually exclusive groups) may see the world through different lenses?

The geography of Australia

Underpinning this book is the belief that looking at the world through a geographical lens has a crucial role to play in pupils' education and in helping them to become informed and active global citizens. We all live on our one planet. Through the media, we frequently see the consequences of our actions and the often awesome effects of Earth's physical actions. We live with the global consequences of these physical events: Iceland's volcanic eruption in 2010 brought airlines worldwide to a virtual standstill and, in January 2011, the La Niña effect, operating off the coast of South America, had devastating consequences even for parts of Queensland, Australia. So how can geography help pupils to gain a better understanding of the world they are growing up in?

Geography's big ideas

Among other things, geography helps us to:
- develop understanding of ourselves and our place in the world
- develop understanding that there are many ways to live in the world
- explore the relationships between people and places and the importance of location in people's lives
- know something of what happens where and why
- develop our understanding that we live in an interconnected world and that our actions (human) and the actions of the planet (physical) can have both beneficial and devastating consequences both for people who live close to us and those who live many thousands of miles away
- understand why caring for our environment and living our lives in a more sustainable way is important for everyone who lives on the planet.

A study of Australia can widen children's perceptions of people and places and support them to ask and answer some key geographical questions, e.g. 'What is this place like?', 'What do people do here?' and 'How does the place influence the lifestyle of the people who live here?'.

The tools of geography

People who study geography use a variety of tools to help them. Sometimes the tools are conflated with the subject, so, for example, geography *is* 'maps', but lots of people use maps of different kinds. For example, an electrician uses a map to help him wire-up a house whereas a geographer might use a map to show the relationships between a place and what people do in that place. In both cases the map provides the format for conveying information spatially. In this book we have tried to show that we need the skills to help pupils understand some of geography's big ideas. It is these big ideas that underpin genuine geographical thinking. Through its toolkit for primary geography teachers this book offers:
- strategies for supporting pupils to ask and answer questions

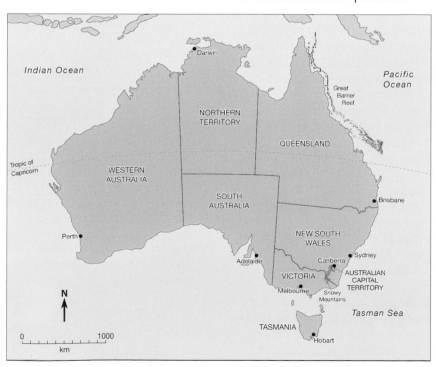

about Australia and for evaluating their answers/data (geographical enquiry)
- an emphasis on looking at Australia using the satellite view of Google Maps, Google Earth or Bing Maps, on representing the world spatially using maps and plans, and on using maps to show relationships between what happens in a place and why
- a wide variety of sources to develop understanding, for example personal accounts, story and photographs; and Google Earth and video to help to create virtual journeys
- key words that support pupils in developing a growing geographical vocabulary.

Using these tools, pupils take on the role of geography explorers and use an enquiry approach to learning. Geography explorers:
- use all the senses
- ask questions
- collect, gather data, information and ideas, then draw and write
- use maps, globes and Google Earth

- show genuine interest in people and places in their own country and the wider world
- share stories of exploration and adventure.

All of these form part of an enquiry approach to learning geography as shown in the diagram on page 32.

Looking at the world using the satellite view on Google Maps (*www.maps.google.com*), Google Earth (*www.google.co.uk/intl/ en_uk/earth*), or Bing Maps (*www.bing.com/maps*) has revolutionised the way we can support pupils to see and experience the world. Pupils' spatial understanding of the world develops through talk and through the many and varied opportunities that they have to see and experience Earth. Using the satellite view, which is the default view of Google Earth and an option in both Google Maps and Bing Maps, pupils can see where countries and places are located. On zooming in for a closer view there is a surprising amount of detail of streets and

houses, something that always delights pupils. Do not forget Google Streetview, (*http://maps. google.com/help/maps/streetview*) with its 360^0 views of places; it is a fabulous way of developing an understanding of 'what places are like', though photographs may be several years old.

It is also important to use 'globe tossing' and atlas maps because these give pupils different and yet complementary hands-on experiences. Maps, globes and atlases in a variety of formats help unlock the door to geographical thinking, skills and knowledge.

Useful links
Further develop your skills and confidence in the use of online mapping by doing one of the online units from the suite of courses on the Geographical Association website at *www.geography.org.uk/cpdevents /onlinecpd/younggeographersgogl obal*.

For more information about the geography of Australia see **Knowledge box 1**.

Lesson/key questions	Learning objectives	Teaching and learning activities	Assessment opportunities	Resources
Lesson 1: Let's Fly to Australia What is Australia like? Where is Australia and how do we get there? What is it like to make such a long journey?	To be able to locate Australia To gain a sense of how far away Australia is from the UK To appreciate how many different landscapes and habitats are contained in this one country	Pupils act out the flight to Australia, returning to take up this activity the following day They investigate Heathrow Airport and draw the interior layout of a plane They record impressions of the 'journey' in a Travel Log	Compare pupils' initial ideas with spoken, drawn and written responses in their travel journals	PowerPoint 1 Photoset 1 Knowledge box 2 World map Travel journals Google Earth
Lesson 2: What should we do in Sydney? What is Sydney like and what can people do there? What makes this city popular with tourists?	To promote a feeling of excitement about Sydney as a place to visit To discover what Sydney is like from a tourist point of view To begin to understand the relationship between the place and what visitors can do there	Pupils explore digital mapping imagery of Australia and Sydney Pupils investigate Sydney locations and put themselves 'in the picture' Pupils describe what you might do on a sightseeing tour	Use pupils' spoken, written and drawn responses to see how well they understand the relationship between the kind of place and what could be done there	Activity sheets 1, 2 and 3 PowerPoint 2 Knowledge box 3 Australia map (copied for each pupil) Travel journals Satellite and aerial views of Sydney from Google Earth or Bing Maps
Lesson 3: What is it like to live in Australia? How are Ethan's life, his place in the world and his environment similar to or different from yours?	To begin to explore the relationship between the environment and what people can do there To know some ways that Ethan's life, his place in the world and his environment are similar to or different from our own	Pupils investigate Ethan's life and describe the activities he does in a typical week then compare with aspects of their own lives Pupils evaluate different places shown in terms of activities that might be done there	Pupils tell each other why a location is/isn't a good place for a particular activity and say what reasons their partner has given	Activity sheets 4, 5 and 6 PowerPoint 3 Photoset 2 Knowledge box 4 Travel journals Bag of artefacts (knee pads, elbow pads, helmet and skateboard) Google Earth or Google Maps
Lesson 4: The sun has got his hat on How will the weather affect what we do today?	To develop understanding of the effects of weather on people and places To develop understanding that weather conditions vary from place to place To be able to follow a route on a Google map	Pupils discuss how to stay safe in the sun and write some advice in their journals Pupils locate the Snowy Mountains and use a card sort activity to identify suitable items to pack for a trip there	Use the card sort activity to assess how well pupils can make connections between weather and location	Activity sheet 7 PowerPoints 3 and 4 Knowledge box 5 Australia map Google Maps *Are We There Yet?* (Lester, 2005)

Lesson/key questions	Learning objectives	Teaching and learning activities	Assessment opportunities	Resources
Lesson 5: Surfing the Waves How does an Australian artist convey a sense of place? How does the artist show what people do in that place?	To recognise different environments To better understand the meaning of a sense of place and be able to use art to communicate it To use own observations to create an image of the coast of New South Wales	Pupils explore different environments within Australia via a storybook Pupils collect patterns and textures and they explore printmaking	Pupils explain to a partner how well their artwork conveys a sense of place and why	Photoset 3 Knowledge box 6 *Malu Kangaroo* (Morecroft and Bancroft, 2008) Printmaking materials (potato, tempera or block printing paint, sponge pads, paper, print rollers, brushes)
Lesson 6: Experiencing Uluru Where is Uluru and what is it like there? How do visiting tourists experience this place? How do the Anangu experience this place?	To respond with a sense of wonder to a new and exciting place To understand that different groups of people may see and 'use' a place in different ways To know that map symbols can convey information	Pupils explore the journey from Sydney to Uluru via maps and aerial images Pupils create story maps to accompany a 'Dreamtime' story Pupils investigate different viewpoints about climbing Uluru	Use pupils' story maps to see how well they know that symbols can convey information Use pupils' explanations about climbing Uluru to see how well they understand that people may have different viewpoints	Activity sheet 8 (Choose from pdf and PowerPoint versions) PowerPoint 5 Knowledge box 7 Australia map Travel journals Sand tray Google Earth
Lesson 7: Coral Reef or Rainforest? Where is this place? What is it like? What creatures live here? What do people do here? How is it changing?	To extend appreciation of the wide variety of landscapes and habitats in Australia To develop locational knowledge of Australia To consider how and why places and environments change and how we can respond	Pupils find and map the locations of the Great Barrier Reef and Daintree rainforest They explore these environments through story, film and photographs and record impressions via journal entries, poetry and/or drama	Use pupils' talk and travel journals to assess how well they can appreciate the diversity of landscapes and use appropriate geographical vocabulary	PowerPoints 1 and 6 Photoset 4 Knowledge box 8 Australia map Travel journals *Finding Nemo* DVD *Curious Clownfish* (Maddern, 1990) *Where the Forest Meets the Sea* (Baker, 1989) Images from Flickr (see Lesson 7 for details)
Lesson 8: What have we learnt and how can we share? What have we learnt about Australia? What do we want to share and why? Who will we share it with and how?	To reinforce, review and assess learning To make choices that explore the relationship between audience and purpose To share learning and benefit from enthusiastic feedback	Pupils select from their journals and learning experiences something they can present to an identified audience	Pupils identify something they have done well and something which they think they could improve	Work from previous lessons Travel journals

Lesson 1: Let's fly to Australia

Key questions
- What is Australia like?
- Where is Australia and how do we get there?
- What is it like to make such a long journey?

Learning objectives
- To be able to locate Australia
- To gain a sense of how far away Australia is from the UK
- To appreciate how many different landscapes and habitats are contained in this one country

Key words
- Coast
- Coral reef
- City
- Desert
- Ocean
- Rainforest

Resources
PowerPoint 1
Photoset 1
Knowledge box 2
World map
Other resources
- Travel journals
- Google Earth

Getting started

This activity will require two lessons approximately 24 hours apart.

Do not tell the pupils what distant place you are going to explore together. Show **PowerPoint 1** and ask 'Where in the world can we find all these in just one amazing country?'. Pause to talk about what excites the pupils in any particular image. (You may choose to use some or all of these images again later in this study.) Pupils may soon start guessing where in the world you are going to explore. Accept all answers. The point is that Australia has some landscapes that could well be in other countries and some that could not possibly be anywhere else. The answer is shown at the end of **PowerPoint 1**.

Main activities
Let's fly to Australia! It's going to take a very long time!

Explain to the pupils that over the next 24 hours they will 'fly to Australia'. On the morning of day one, project images from **Photoset 1** of Heathrow Airport and talk about what this huge airport is like and what people do there. This could be an opportunity for a role play. Then project the image of the inside of a long-haul airliner. Ask the pupils if they can see how the seats are arranged; they might be able to draw a plan of this interior. They then need to set out enough chairs for the class in the right formation facing the whiteboard.

When pupils arrive the next morning they return to their 'plane seats'. Tell pupils that they have been flying around the

world towards Australia all night and show them the route on Google Earth (*www.google.com/earth*). Now zoom in slowly on the coast of New South Wales and then Sydney Airport as the plane 'lands'. Ask the pupils to describe what they can see as they fly lower and lower, then land.

Drama and question sequences, and ideas for props and organisational approaches to make this experience 'come alive' are given in **Knowledge box 2.** Pupils should leave this experience with an understanding that it takes a long, long time to travel to Australia, even by air. The use of Google Earth will enable pupils to locate Australia.

Travel journal

Throughout this unit pupils will keep a travel journal as a record of their learning. It could be a folder or a large exercise book – pupils could make their own. It is a place where pupils can keep 'stuff' that helps them to think through, remember, and reflect on what they are learning. It could even be the shared product of a small group, with each pupil making a contribution. There is guidance on using the travel journals in **Knowledge box 2.** Following on from the 'flight' and 'arrival' in Australia, ask pupils to use their travel journals to draw, write and map their responses to this part of their journey,

choosing what to record and how to record it. They could start with the **World map** to locate the UK and Australia.

Plenary

Share what pupils have recorded in their journals. Talk about any aspect of the flight that has been of interest and answer questions. Some questions can be saved for future discussion.

Extension

The saying that 'the shortest distance between two points is a straight line' is not always true! The curvature of Earth means that if the aircraft takes a curved trajectory it will travel less distance, and thus consume less fuel than if it flew in a straight line. Pupils could check this using a globe and a length of wool or string.

What next?

You may want to start thinking together now about organising an event to share the outcomes of the journey with the rest of the school and parents, for example about how images and readings could be presented, as this will be the focus of Lesson 8.

All references and websites for this lesson are listed on the **Further information** sheet.

Lesson 2: What should we do in S

Sydney

Key questions
- What is Sydney like and what can people do there?
- What makes this city popular with tourists?

Learning objectives
- To promote a feeling of excitement about Sydney as a place to visit
- To discover what Sydney is like from a tourist point of view
- To begin to understand the relationship between the place and what visitors can do there

Key words
- Aerial
- Beach
- City
- Harbour
- Landmark
- Leisure
- Satellite view
- Settlement
- Tourism

Resources
Activity sheets
1: If I was in the picture
2: What Jack and Charlotte did
3: This is what they saw
PowerPoint 2
Knowledge box 3
Australia map (copied for each pupil)
Other resources
- Travel journals
- Satellite and aerial views of Sydney from Google Earth or Bing Maps

Getting started
This lesson will look at Sydney through the eyes of two children from Sheffield. Jack and Charlotte undertook an amazing world holiday with their mum ('Hils') and dad ('the Captain') in 2009. First they visited the USA, then Australia and then New Zealand.

Using online mapping, locate Australia and then Sydney and investigate the different views available, such as bird's eye and aerial on Bing Maps (*www.bing.com/maps/*) or the satellite view on Google Maps (*http://maps.google.co.uk/*). Talk with pupils about what they can see and explain to them that very

large settlements like Sydney are cities. Pupils can locate Sydney on their copy of the **Australia map** to stick in their travel journals.

Main activities
Pick a place
PowerPoint 2 tells the story of the two days that Jack and Charlotte spent in Sydney. The PowerPoint has been designed as a 'choose your own adventure' activity using hyperlinks. Pupils are asked to choose from six places that Jack and Charlotte might visit while they are in Sydney. When the class has decided, click on the image and follow Jack and Charlotte's visit. Further information about Sydney can be found in **Knowledge box 3**.

After viewing the slides on the chosen location in Sydney ask pupils to use **Activity sheet 1** to put themselves in that place and use their senses to describe what they can see and what they can hear.

Exploring Sydney
After working through all of **PowerPoint 2** pupils could

complete **Activity sheets 2** and **3** using words and pictures to show what Jack and Charlotte did and saw during their sightseeing in Sydney.

Plenary

Re-visit the Google Map or Bing Map to locate all the places that Jack and Charlotte visited. Show pupils how to find places on the map by typing the venue into the search box, e.g. Sydney Aquarium. Zoom in and look carefully at the location and what it is like. Ask your pupils to think what makes this a good location for the particular venue.

Pupils can write and draw in their travel journal about their visit to Sydney. You might ask them to think about which is their favourite place in Sydney and why.

Extension activity

ICT-confident pupils could explore **PowerPoint 2** in pairs. They could find out more about a particular location, for example Sydney Aquarium or the Sydney Tower. When they have chosen three things that they especially liked they could share this with the rest of the class.

What next?

Sydney is just one of the places that Jack and Charlotte visited during their holiday. Your pupils may like to see more of their adventures by exploring their website (*http://web.me.com/ian read/Readsontour/Welcome.html*) or to use the picture book *Are we there yet?* (Lester, 2005), which describes the adventures of an Australian family who take a term off school to travel around Australia.

Sydney, the state capital of New South Wales, is the largest and most heavily populated settlement in Australia. It has the biggest natural harbour in the world. In 1770 Captain James Cook landed in Botany Bay, a few kilometres south of the centre of modern Sydney. He made contact with the aboriginal people who are thought to have lived there for at least 40,000 years. In 1778 a colony was established for convicts from Britain. Soon after, an outbreak of smallpox wiped out thousands of aboriginal people.

Geography
Knowledge and understanding
- Place, space and scale

Enquiry and skills
- Use appropriate geographical vocabulary to ask questions and respond
- Communicate in different ways
- Use maps and plans
- Use images to develop a sense of place

Plus
English
Speaking and listening:
- acquiring new vocabulary
Writing:
- sentences using descriptive vocabulary

ICT
- Using PowerPoint and digital imaging
- Using online mapping

Assessment opportunities

Use pupils' spoken, written and drawn responses to see how well they understand the relationship between the kind of place and what could be done there.

Geography, taught well, helps pupils to understand what places are like; why they are like they are and what the relationship is between the place and what people do there.

All references and websites for this lesson are listed on the **Further information** sheet.

The Entrance

Key questions

- How are Ethan's life, his place in the world and his environment similar to or different from yours?

Learning objectives

- To begin to explore the relationship between the environment and what people can do there
- To know some ways that Ethan's life, his place in the world and his environment are similar to or different from our own

Key words

- Coast
- Lake
- Leisure
- Resort
- Sea
- Village

Resources

Activity sheets
- 4: Who am I?
- 5: What can people do here?
- 6: A good or not so good place?

PowerPoint 3
Photoset 2
Knowledge box 4
Australia map
Other resources
- Travel journals
- Bag of artefacts (knee pads, elbow pads, helmet and skateboard)
- Google Earth or Google Maps

Getting started

Produce the artefacts from your bag one by one – can pupils work out what activity they will be talking about today and who might feature in the 'story'? Where in the world might the story be set?

Show the images from **Photoset 2** of the skateboard park with lake and pelicans to help pupils think about who might feature in our next story and whether (s)he lives in the UK or Australia.

Main activities

Where in the world is Ethan?

The boy in the photos is four-year-old Ethan. He lives near The Entrance, a coastal resort on the Central Coast of New South Wales, 105km north of Sydney. Locate The Entrance using Google Earth or Google Maps and ask the pupils to mark it on their copy of the **Australia map.**

What does Ethan do there?

Use **PowerPoint 3** to tell the story of Ethan's week and explore the questions: Who is Ethan? What is his story? What is his place like? What can he do in this place? How does he feel about the different activities he takes part in during the week? The PowerPoint slides for Monday, Tuesday, Wednesday and Thursday show the local area where Ethan lives, using hyperlinks. Help your pupils to explore what Ethan can do here. The skateboard activity is

done on Wednesday. At the weekend, Ethan and his family visit the Snowy Mountains and Canberra. In **Knowledge box 4** you will find background information about Ethan and his life and helpful question prompts.

Use **Activity sheet 4** to prompt thinking about identity: pupils think about aspects of Ethan's life and their own life.

Why is that done there?
Some of the slides in **PowerPoint 3** show other people taking part in different activities in the area. Ask pupils to use **Activity sheets 5** and **6** to record what other people do there. What makes it a good location for these activities? It is important to ask pupils to say why they think this is a good or not very good place for the activity. They could do this with a talking partner if they are not confident writers.

Mapping Ethan's life
Knowledge box 4 gives detailed activity guidance to help you create a large floor map of the area and locate where Ethan lives and the places he visits.

All references and websites for this lesson are listed on the **Further information** sheet.

Plenary
The pupils complete a travel journal entry. On one side of a double page, under the heading 'Meeting Ethan', they draw, or draw and write about, some of the things that Ethan enjoys doing during the week. On the opposite page, under the heading 'Meeting me', they draw, or draw and write about, some of the activities that they enjoy doing. Use **Activity sheet 4** as a guide.

Discuss surprises about Ethan's life, such as the weekend activities of making snowmen and tobogganing in the Snowy Mountains.

What next?
Encourage pupils to talk about the similarities and differences between their own week and Ethan's. They could share some of their journal pages with each other. This should help them to see that there are lots of differences between the way they each spend their time and that difference is not just about living in a distant place.

Ask pupils to think about where they might prefer to live and give reasons why. Would they like their families to live on the coast of Australia or are they happy to live where they do now?

Geography
Knowledge and understanding
- Place, space and scale

Enquiry and skills
- Use secondary sources of information
- Make maps and plans
- Identify and describe what places are like

Plus
English
Speaking and listening:
- Ask questions, use descriptive vocabulary
- Write captions

History
- Talk about our own families and 'who we are'

Assessment opportunities
Activity sheets 5 and **6** ask pupils to say if a particular place is a good location for a particular activity. Using peer assessment, pupils can report back as to whether their partner gave good reasons and what these were for the choices they were asked to make.

The Central Coast of New South Wales is around an hour's drive (105km) north of Sydney. It is a popular holiday destination with golden beaches, National Parks and coastal settlements. The Entrance lies just north of the small coastal city of Gosford in Wyongshire. It has a waterfront park, beaches and lakes.

Lesson 4: The sun has got his hat

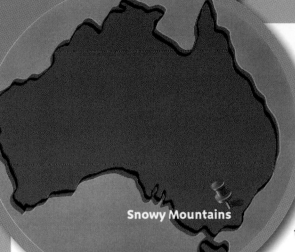

Snowy Mountains

Key questions
- How will the weather affect what we do today?

Learning objectives
- To develop understanding of the effects of weather on people and places
- To develop understanding that weather conditions vary from place to place
- To be able to follow a route on a Google Map

Key words
- Ice
- Journey
- Mountain
- Route
- Sail shades
- Snow

Resources
Activity sheet
   7: What should Ethan take to the Snowy Mountains?
PowerPoint 3
PowerPoint 4
Knowledge box 5
Australia map
Other resources
- Google Maps
- *Are We There Yet?* (Lester, 2005)

Getting started
Show pupils **PowerPoint 3** from the last lesson, focusing particularly on Monday to Thursday. Ask your pupils to be 'geography detectives' and spot as many ways as they can that people protect themselves from the damaging effects of the sun. Ask them to recall (from the last session) the activities that people can do here on the coast. How does the sun affect the people who take part in these activities? How do they take care in the sun? **Knowledge box 5** gives some background information about weather and climate in Australia.

Main activities
The sun has got his hat on
Pupils discuss with 'talking partners' the best way to help a friend from the UK to take care in the sun. They then create a page for their journals, possibly a letter of advice to their friend, to show some ways to take care in the sun.

Set up an area with all the items that pupils will need to take care of themselves in the sun. What will they wear? What might be sold in the beach shop? What might be sold in the pharmacy?

Off to the snow!
The Snowy Mountains of New South Wales provide a contrasting locality to the Central Coast. Use **PowerPoint 4** to follow the route that Ethan and his family took in order to get from their home, near The Entrance, to the Snowy Mountains. Pupils can locate the Snowy Mountains on their **Australia map**.

Ethan is packing his bag
The card sort on **Activity sheet 7** provides an opportunity for pupils to discuss and share higher level thinking about the impact of weather on people and place. You can use it as an assessment opportunity to review pupils' understanding. Copy the sheet and cut the items up into separate cards (you may decide to select fewer items for younger pupils). Pupils work with a partner to choose ten (or fewer) cards which are items they would pack for Ethan's trip. Pupils should record the items they choose in their travel journals.

Are we there yet?

Read *Are we there yet?* (Lester, 2005). This tells the story of a family trip around Australia. Use the story to explore the different kinds of weather conditions the family encounter on their journey.

Plenary

Encourage pupils to talk about the similarities and differences between the coast and the mountain environment. They might choose to share their journal pages about keeping safe in the sun or to show another pair of pupils which items they think Ethan would pack in his rucksack.

Extension

Pupils could draw people wearing the most appropriate clothes for the weather in each part of Australia. These could then be displayed on an enlarged copy of the **Australia map**.

What next?

Ask pupils to think about where they might like to go on holiday in Australia. Would they prefer the coast of Australia or the Snowy Mountains? Why?

Geography
Knowledge and understanding
- Place, space and scale
- Human and physical processes: weather

Enquiry and skills
- Ask geographical questions
- Use maps
- Express views
- Compare places with other places

Plus
English
Speaking and listening:
- Discussing similarities and differences
- Using descriptive vocabulary
- Write lists
- Drama in a role-play area

Assessment opportunities
Use the card sort activity on **Activity sheet 7** to assess how well pupils are making connections between location and variation in weather.

Mount Kosciuszko, Australia.

Geography, taught well, helps pupils to understand the way the physical environment impacts on people and places. In this lesson we focus on the effect of weather on people and how it influences the type of activities that people can do in a place.

Mount Kosciuszko is 2228m above sea level. It is the highest mountain in Australia (not including its external territories). This is much higher than any mountain in the UK.

SunSmart campaign:
- Slip on sun protective clothing
- Slop on SPF 30+ sunscreen
- Slap on a hat
- Seek shade
- Slide on some sunglasses
More details from the Cancer Council of Australia:
www.cancer.org.au/cancersm artlifestyle/cancersmartlifesty lefactsheets/Be_sunsmart.htm

All references and websites for this lesson are listed on the **Further information** sheet.

Lesson 5: Surfing the waves

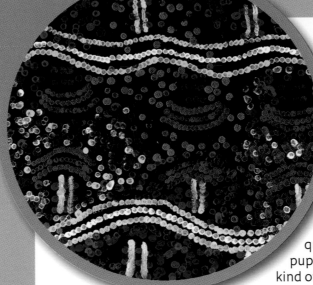

Key questions
- How does an Australian artist convey a sense of place?
- How does the artist show what people do in that place?

Learning objectives
- To recognise different environments
- To better understand the meaning of a sense of place
- To be able to use art to communicate a sense of place
- To use own observations to create an image of the coast of New South Wales

Key words
- Bush
- Coast
- Patterns
- Print
- Sea
- Surf
- Waves

Resources
Photoset 3
Knowledge box 6
Other resources
- *Malu Kangaroo* (Morecroft and Bancroft, 2008)
- Printmaking materials (potato, tempera or block printing paint, sponge pads, paper, print rollers, brushes)

Getting started
Take a virtual journey along the Wyrrabalong trail using the images in **Photoset 3**. The trail is in a National Park on the Central Coast of New South Wales. The pupils need to imagine that they are walking along the beach and then along the coastal path. What do they see, hear, smell and feel on their skin in this place? Follow this up with a discussion about their journey. This could be extended into an activity to create a picture map in their travel journal.

Main activities
Telling a story
Malu Kangaroo (Morecroft and Bancroft, 2008) is a modern retelling of the story of how people first learnt to surf, set in a real place on the northern coast of New South Wales. As you read the story, use prompt questions to engage your pupils with the artwork: What kind of place does the artist show us through her paintings? What would you expect to find in this place? What would you see, hear, smell and feel on your skin in this place? What is the sea like here? Ask the pupils to think about how the pictures make them feel. Perhaps they will feel excited by the large waves pounding the beach and by the bright colours and sense of light.

Develop the art
You can support pupils to develop genuine artistic thinking and skills if you run these art activities over several weeks. The main focus of the activities in this

session is on developing pupils' understanding of artistic pattern through print-making.

Use *Malu Kangaroo* to explore the rich and intricate artwork, comparing the shapes and patterns on different pages. Pupils then collect patterns and textures in the school environment and make sketches.

They take this activity further by developing designs to represent what they think coastal Australia is like. They could build print patterns using a range of materials, such as potatoes, small blocks or print rollers, or they could print images using polystyrene. **Knowledge box 6** has a detailed step-by-step guide to these activities.

Plenary
Ask the pupils to identify what the patterns represent and compare the different patterns in their work. How is their work similar to or different from the work created by Bronwyn Bancroft in *Malu Kangaroo*?

Extension activity
Bronwyn Bancroft adapts her style to the purpose of the different books she illustrates. Pupils could look at some of her other books to see how the illustrations convey a sense of place and how they change to suit audience and purpose.

What next?
Create a gallery display of their paintings for the pupils to guide their visitors around, explaining how they were created and how they feel about their images. This can be an element of the final presentation of this work to an audience.

Geography
Knowledge and understanding
- Place, space and scale: developing a sense of place

Enquiry and skills
- Use geographical vocabulary to explain what images show
- Communicate in different ways, for example through art

Plus
English
Speaking and listening:
- Describe and explain what is seen

Maths
- Making and identifying patterns

Art
- Exploring and developing ideas
- Investigating and making
- Evaluating and developing

Assessment opportunities
Ask pupils to think about how well their work conveys a sense of place and explain it to a partner.

Geography, taught well, helps pupils to understand about places and environments. Art can help to widen our understanding of what places are like. Artists can interpret places in a very personal way, often focused on conveying a 'sense of place' and on showing what the artist 'feels' rather than on showing photographic reality.

Bronwyn Bancroft paints her images using brushes though she does appear to print the dots. For more information about her work visit: *www.bronwynbancroft.com*

All references and websites for this lesson are listed on the **Further information** sheet.

Many artists use a mixture of techniques to create images. Pupils may like to explore the patterns in Aboriginal art. Examples can be seen at: Aboriginal Australia Art and Culture Centre, Alice Springs (*http://aboriginalart.com.au/culture/dreamtime2.html*) and Aboriginal Art Online (*www.aboriginalartonline.com/culture/symbols.php/*).

Lesson 6: Experiencing Uluru

Uluru

Key questions
- Where is Uluru and what is it like there?
- How do visiting tourists experience this place?
- How do the Anangu experience this place?

Learning objectives
- To respond with a sense of wonder to a new and exciting place
- To understand that different groups of people may see and 'use' a place in different ways
- To know that map symbols can convey information

Key words
- Aboriginal
- Anangu
- Dreamtime
- Uluru

Resources
Activity sheet
   8: To climb or not to climb? (Available as an activity sheet and as a PowerPoint activity)
PowerPoint 5
Knowledge box 7
Australia map
Other resources
- Travel journals
- Sand tray
- Google Earth

Getting started
Uluru is as far away from the coast as it is possible to get in Australia. To drive there across the desert takes about four days; it takes three-and-a-half hours to fly. Considering this will give pupils some idea of the vastness of the country.

Ask pupils to mark the flight path from Sydney to Uluru on the map in their travel journals. With their talking partners they can discuss what they think they might see from the plane on the flight, and make a couple of brief notes or a quick sketch in a plane-window-shaped frame in their travel journals.

Use Google Earth to show the pupils what they would actually see. Project the flight from Sydney to the Red Centre on the white board and 'fly' very slowly, zooming out as the plane leaves Sydney and zooming in as it lands. Allow the pupils to share what they can see and elicit the changes from an urban environment to the desert. Fly in low circles over Uluru and its 'tourist resort' while the pupils pick out the different things they can see there (red rocks, bright green grass, various buildings, bright blue swimming pool).

Wally, our Anangu Ranger, is waiting for Katya to finish translating part of the story of Blue-tongue Lizard Man (Lungkata) and Crested Bellbird Man (Panpanpalala) he has just told and mapped in the sand. In a minute he will take his spear back and continue the story in Pitjanjara, his own language. The tourists are listening: Lizard Man has stolen the sleeping Bellbird Man's emu meat and they want to know what's going to happen next!

Main activities

Sense impressions

Ask pupils to choose three sense impressions each from their memories of this flight to note or draw in their travel journal.

Where do visitors stay?

Explore the tourist resort, built in the hottest, driest part of Australia, known as the Red Centre. Project the Yulara website *www.ayersrockresort.com.au* to show what is available to visitors. What is it like here? What do tourists do here? What has had to happen here to supply what tourists expect? Pupils should choose a tourist activity they would like to do and note or draw it in their travel journal.

A dreamtime story

PowerPoint 5 shows Wally, an Anangu Ranger, who tells tourists the Dreamtime story of *Lungkata and Panpanpalala* to help them understand what this place means to his people. He tells the story using mapping diagrams. **Knowledge box 7** gives Wally's view of Uluru with the full text of the story as well as some background information about Dreamtime stories. Either tell the story from memory, drawing the map for your pupils in sand, or read them the text while showing the story map slides in **PowerPoint 5**.

Using story maps

Some pupils will be able to tell the story using the completed story map, and some may be able to draw the map, either in sand or on a large piece of paper, as they narrate. Any journey story can be mapped in this way. Pupils could go on to invent their own symbols to map a story they know well.

To climb or not to climb?

Some tourists are less concerned than others with respecting the beliefs of the Anangu – they want to climb to the top of the rock for the stunning view. There are images of climbers and the footpath up Uluru on **PowerPoint 5**. You have to look closely to find the tiny 'ants', as climbers are called by the Aboriginals. Read out the comments on **Activity sheet 8** or on the PowerPoint version one at a time and ask the pupils to say whether they think the person speaking is an Anangu or a tourist. Ask the pupils to discuss with a talking partner whether they would climb Uluru, and why or why not, and then share their views.

Plenary

Share some additions to travel journals. Plan together what you might add to your final event from this lesson. Perhaps your pupils could tell their audience a story from a story map.

What next?

Explore more sophisticated story maps, such as *Tjarany Roughtail* (Greene *et al.*, 1992). This shows what happens to aboriginal story mapping when drawing in the sand is extended into more permanent painting and book illustration. Further ideas to develop thinking about places that are special to certain groups are given in **Knowledge box 7**.

Geography
Knowledge and understanding
- Place, space and scale
- Culture and diversity

Enquiry and skills
- Express own views
- Use stories
- Make maps and plans

Plus
English
- Read and tell stories
- Take part in group discussions
- Write notes

ICT
- Use digital audio and video recording

Assessment opportunities

Use pupils' own story maps: how well do they understand that symbols convey information? Use pupils' explanations about whether they would climb Uluru or not to assess how well they are beginning to understand different viewpoints.

Uluru, in Australia's Northern Territory, is the world's largest rock outcrop. The sandstone rock is 348m high and 2.4km long. In 1873 European explorers named Uluru Ayers Rock after the then Chief Secretary of South Australia. Uluru has great cultural significance for the traditional landowners, the Anangu.

All references and websites for this lesson are listed on the **Further information** sheet.

Lesson 7: Coral reef or rainforest?

Daintree
Great Barrier Reef

Key questions
- Where is this place?
- What is it like?
- What creatures live here?
- What do people do here?
- How is it changing?

Learning objectives
- To extend appreciation of the wide variety of landscapes and habitats in Australia
- To develop locational knowledge of Australia
- To consider how and why places and environments change and how we can respond

Key words
- Coral reef
- Rainforest
- Sea
- Tropical

Resources
PowerPoint 1
PowerPoint 6
Knowledge box 8
Photoset 4
Australia map
Other resources
- Travel journals
- *Finding Nemo* DVD
- *Curious Clownfish* (Maddern, 1990)
- *Where the Forest Meets the Sea* (Baker, 1989)
- Images from Flickr (see URL in text)

Getting started
Using **PowerPoint 1**, recap with pupils the different types of Australian landscape you have explored together so far. This lesson explores two more exciting places through picture books: the Great Barrier Reef and the Daintree Rainforest. Both are in Queensland. Ask pupils to explain what a rainforest is and what they think the Great Barrier Reef is. You may choose to focus on only one of these locations.

Main activities
At the Great Barrier Reef
Zoom over the Great Barrier Reef using Google Earth and ask pupils to mark it on their Australia map in their travel journals. The Great Barrier Reef is the largest coral reef in the world (see **Knowledge box 8** for further information).

The opening of the Disney film *Finding Nemo* gives a strong impression of the variety of coral reef life, interpreted by animation artists. Then read *Curious Clownfish* (Madden, 1990). **PowerPoint 6** has some links to YouTube videos that show people scuba diving at the Reef.

Travel journals
Ask pupils to record in their travel journals, in notes or drawings, the colours, shapes, creatures and plants of the coral reef that they find most exciting. In **Photoset 4** there are also some images taken by a tourist with an underwater camera while snorkelling on the Great Barrier Reef.

Shared writing
Show the class the set of pictures at *www.flickr.com/photos/leonardlow/sets/72157594451583604/* showing the fish of the Great Barrier Reef. Watch the images as a slideshow, pausing occasionally for discussion.

While showing these images, ask the pupils to imagine that they are diving there and ask each pupil in turn to complete the sentence-opener 'I can see...' orally. Scribe their responses on the board to create a poem. You can edit this as a whole class for a group performance later, adding other elements, such as the

exciting names of the various fish. **Knowledge box 8** has an example of a poem by a year 1 class.

At the Daintree Rainforest
Zoom over the Daintree Rainforest using Google Earth, and ask pupils to mark it on their Australia map in their travel journals. Use the images in **Photoset 3** to show pupils the characteristics of a rainforest (see **Knowledge box 8** for further information).

Performance response
Read *Where the Forest Meets the Sea* (Baker, 1989), set in the Daintree rainforest, as a stimulus to develop a performance response. You will need a space in which the pupils can spread out. Read each page, commenting on those details in the pictures that are not expressed in the text, and ask pupils to perform the boy's actions to get the feel of how he moves, what he feels on his skin, etc.

There are ideas for developing this drama in **Knowledge box 8**. It could be developed into a performance piece to share, possibly continuing with the clearing of the ancient forest and the construction of hotels and other developments.

Travel journals
In their travel journals, pupils could note four detailed sense impressions from their 'walk' in the rainforest, or sketch some of the creepers/roots they 'found' there and fill a whole page with the patterns they make. Or you could ask pupils what they found most magical about the rainforest and to add labelled sketches or notes to their journals.

Plenary
Ask pupils to think about the landscape they have studied through story and think of a sentence to describe it. Share responses, identifying good points and possible improvements. Ask pupils what they would really want to remember about this special place.

Extension activity
On her website *(www.jeanniebaker.com)* Jeannie Baker gives two brief descriptions of how she constructs the artwork that becomes the pictures in her books. She translates her photographs into textured collages which are then photographed. Pupils could choose an image of the rainforest and re-express this in texture, choosing from a range of materials.

What next?
Challenge pupils to carry out their own research on either of the landscapes studied through these stories.

All references and websites for this lesson are listed on the **Further information** sheet.

Coral reefs are found in shallow tropical waters. Corals are colonies of tiny living animals called polyps. At their base is a hard, protective limestone skeleton called a calicle, which forms the structure of coral reefs. The polyp calicles connect to one another, creating a colony. As colonies grow over thousands of years, they join with other colonies and become reefs. Some of the coral reefs on the planet today began growing over 50 million years ago.

Lesson 8: What have we learnt ar

Key questions
- What have we learnt about Australia?
- What do we want to share and why?
- Who will we share it with and how?

Learning objectives
- To reinforce, review and assess learning
- To make choices that explore the relationship between audience and purpose
- To share learning and benefit from enthusiastic feedback

Key words
- Audience
- Purpose

Resources
- Work from previous lessons
- Travel journals

Getting started
Throughout the lessons in this journey round Australia it has been suggested that pupils will review what they have learned and select elements to share with others.

A piece of creative work begins with an exciting idea, which is then researched, extended, developed and refined until it can be shared with an audience. The enquiry framework on page 32 sets out this process.

Discuss with the pupils who their audience might be. Draw up a list of suggestions and discuss which ones are reasonable. The list might include: another class, or other classes, in school; parents and friends of your class; a class from your local secondary school; older people from your community; your governors; or any combination of these. Perhaps you have a member of the Geographical Association in your school, or a local geography adviser, inspector, or Initial Teacher Educator and trainee teachers? Who else can you think of?

Main activities
You can make the organisation of this event as easy or challenging for yourself and your pupils as you like, from inviting the class next-door to come and watch and listen for half-an-hour, to designing invitations and baking kangaroo biscuits for an event. Have fun!

Inviting your audience
Discuss with your pupils how to approach your identified audience. For example, should it be by phone, email or a formal written invitation? Who will do this?

Choosing what to share and how
Next, brainstorm a list of what might be shared. This could be whatever you and your pupils choose from all your explorations of Australia together. For example, pupils could:
- take their audience on a role-play flight and locate important places on a map

- guide their visitors around a gallery of their art-work, displayed travel journals and other work
- show some images of Australia from the places and activities they have studied and tell their audience about them
- show one of the hyperlinked PowerPoint presentations that shows children visiting Sydney or living on the Central Coast of New South Wales and encourage their audience to choose one aspect which the pupils could then explain
- tell their audience the Dreamtime tale of Blue-tongue Lizard Man and Crested Bellbird Man with a story map
- show their audience their drama piece, with sound effects as they walk through the Daintree Rainforest, against a backdrop of projected rainforest images
- take their audience on a virtual visit to the Great Barrier Reef and perform their sense impression poems.

The pupils could select work from any of the previous lessons, as long as it meets the criteria relating to audience: they must think about the age of their audience, what will interest them, and the purpose of the event, which is to help the audience to enjoy the event and understand as much as possible about Australia.

Taking part
Decide as a class who will do what and allocate roles. For example, different groups might present different pieces of work, some may be responsible for posting/sending/emailing invitations or for organising props, etc.

Designing invitations
You may wish to send formal invitations, with an Australian theme, that the pupils can design and make.

Plenary
After the event, discuss what pupils feel most proud of and why. Ask them to identify something they did especially well and something they would like to have done better.

This event will also provide a final opportunity for assessment – a time to review how individual pupils and groups have changed and developed in the course of this study, in relation to the learning objectives. How well have they understood and absorbed the complex place that is 'Australia'? What do they show that they can do now, that they could not do (so well) at the beginning?

What next?
Compile various examples of work from this experience for the school website.

Assessment opportunities
Use work produced by pupils, together with their comments about which work should be selected for the final event to see how well they have reflected on their learning.

All references and websites for this lesson are listed on the **Further information** sheet.

Further teaching ideas

Focus on asking questions about photographs

This activity could provide you with a starting point for pupil-led enquiry learning. However, some of the questions that pupils ask are often very narrow. One strategy is to ask: 'Can we park these questions for now and then come back to them and discuss which ones could lead us to finding out more interesting things about this place and what people can do here?'.

Images are a very good way to engage pupils and prompt enquiry questions. The aim of this teaching idea is to encourage pupils to ask their own questions about a photograph. It requires a collection of photographs and some prompt cards with the key question words shown below:

It is important that the pupils have previous experience of asking geographical questions in relation to photographs before they try this activity for themselves.

Organise your class into pairs and give each pair a photograph. Hold up a prompt card with 'What?' written on it. Ask if anyone can ask their partner a question about their photograph that starts with the word 'what'. Ask if the partner understood the question and was able to give an answer. Was it a good question? Look for feedback from your class.

Repeat the activity for other key question words.

To develop this activity, encourage pairs of pupils to work independently. Ask pupils to write out their questions on slips of card or dry-wipe boards so that they can show other members of the class. Finally, choose a question that will make a suitable focus for a whole-class enquiry.

What?	Where?	Why?
Who?	When?	How?

Concepts covered

Geographical concepts: ways of organising knowledge

Concepts are big ideas about the subject. They are not definitive but give a framework for organising subject knowledge. In primary geography, place, space and scale are often viewed together as the most relevant concepts for underpinning quality work and can be enhanced to deepen understanding by building in some other big ideas. All of these concepts are fundamental aspects of geographical knowledge and understanding, however, so will endure future curriculum change.

All the *Geography Plus* resources are underpinned by space, place and scale, yet will differ in the prominence they give to some of the other big ideas of geography. There is nothing to stop you adapting the given foci if you wish to develop the learning through a different geographical lens.

The activities in this book promote creativity, thinking skills and ICT capability.

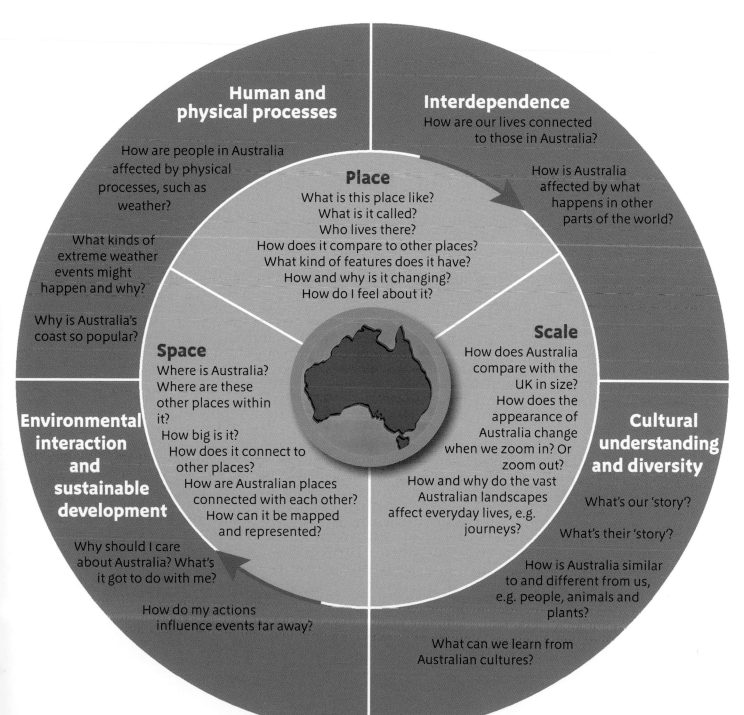

Human and physical processes
How are people in Australia affected by physical processes, such as weather?
What kinds of extreme weather events might happen and why?
Why is Australia's coast so popular?

Interdependence
How are our lives connected to those in Australia?
How is Australia affected by what happens in other parts of the world?

Place
What is this place like?
What is it called?
Who lives there?
How does it compare to other places?
What kind of features does it have?
How and why is it changing?
How do I feel about it?

Space
Where is Australia?
Where are these other places within it?
How big is it?
How does it connect to other places?
How are Australian places connected with each other?
How can it be mapped and represented?

Scale
How does Australia compare with the UK in size?
How does the appearance of Australia change when we zoom in? Or zoom out?
How and why do the vast Australian landscapes affect everyday lives, e.g. journeys?

Environmental interaction and sustainable development
Why should I care about Australia? What's it got to do with me?
How do my actions influence events far away?

Cultural understanding and diversity
What's our 'story'?
What's their 'story'?
How is Australia similar to and different from us, e.g. people, animals and plants?
What can we learn from Australian cultures?

An enquiry framework

When deciding how to adapt any of the activities in this book, whether for an individual lesson or as part of a new unit of work, you may find it helpful to refer to these enquiry prompts.

Collaborating
Working together, how will we find out...?
Which are the best questions?
Where will we find answers?
What resources can we use?
How will we do this?

Asking
Use a mix of given and pupils' own questions as a starting point:
What do I already know?
What do I think I know?
What do I want to know?
What vocabulary do I need?

Choosing skills, techniques and resources
How will we analyse and present information? For example:
Data loggers? Video?
Stories? Reports?
Graphs? Tables?
Pictures? Drama?

Attitudes and values

Starting knowledge

Skills

Creativity

New and emerging knowledge

Critical thinking

Reflecting
What have we found out?
What does it mean?
How does this affect my life?
How do I feel about...?
Do we all share the same point of view?

Evaluating
**What have we learnt?
How do we know?
Has it changed our thinking?
If so, how?
For example:**
Through self- and peer-assessment activities

What new questions do we have?

What next?

Communicating
**What do we do with this knowledge?
Who can we share it with?
And how? For example:**
Feedback to each other in class
Use school website
Do presentations to other classes
Assemblies
Send newsletters to parents
Write letters to the local press and MP

Assessment and progression

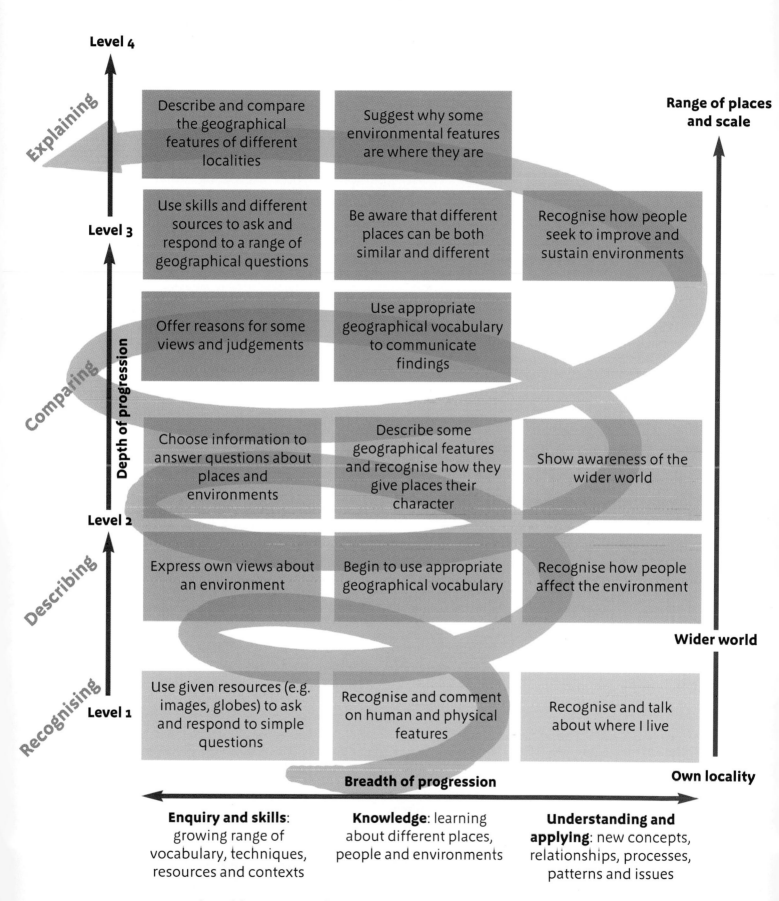

Level 4

Explaining

Describe and compare the geographical features of different localities

Suggest why some environmental features are where they are

Range of places and scale

Level 3

Use skills and different sources to ask and respond to a range of geographical questions

Be aware that different places can be both similar and different

Recognise how people seek to improve and sustain environments

Comparing

Depth of progression

Offer reasons for some views and judgements

Use appropriate geographical vocabulary to communicate findings

Choose information to answer questions about places and environments

Describe some geographical features and recognise how they give places their character

Show awareness of the wider world

Level 2

Describing

Express own views about an environment

Begin to use appropriate geographical vocabulary

Recognise how people affect the environment

Wider world

Recognising

Level 1

Use given resources (e.g. images, globes) to ask and respond to simple questions

Recognise and comment on human and physical features

Recognise and talk about where I live

Own locality

Breadth of progression

| **Enquiry and skills**: growing range of vocabulary, techniques, resources and contexts | **Knowledge**: learning about different places, people and environments | **Understanding and applying**: new concepts, relationships, processes, patterns and issues |

For examples of formative and summative assessment in practice see
www.geography.org.uk/cpdevents/onlinecpd/primarysubjectleadership/assessment

Glossary

Aboriginal – earliest or original inhabitants of the land

Aerial – view as seen from above or from the air

Anangu – traditional aboriginal owners

Audience – the people being addressed by an event, performance, book, film or play

Beach – an accumulation of sand and shingle material at a coast or at the edge of a body of water

Bush – a rural area in Australia, also called the Outback; anywhere that is not in town

City – an urban area where a large number of people live and work

Coast – the land beside the sea

Coral reef – offshore accumulation of dead coral, usually with live coral on top

Desert – an area of land with an annual rainfall of 250mm or less

Dreamtime – The time of the creation of the world in Aboriginal mythology

Harbour – a port where ships can safely shelter while they take on or unload cargo

Ice – frozen water

Journey – travelling from one place to another

Lake – an inland body of fresh water

Landmark – a prominent, identifying feature of a landscape

Leisure – time free from work or other commitments to engage in recreational activities

Mountain – a natural, large elevation of Earth's surface rising abruptly from the surrounding area. In Britain this normally refers to an elevation exceeding 600m above sea level

Ocean – a large expanse of sea. The five main oceans are the Atlantic, Pacific, Indian, Arctic and Southern Oceans. They cover 71% of Earth's surface

Patterns – repeated decorative designs

Print – to create a picture or design using inked blocks or plates

Purpose – intention, or something to be attained

Rainforest – a dense forest, comprising tall trees, growing in areas of very high rainfall. Rainforest is found in some temperate regions but is most typical of tropical regions

Resort – a place frequented by people for relaxation or recreation

Route – a road, course, or way for travel from one place to another

Sail shades – sail-shaped covers used outdoors to provide shelter from the sun and rain

Satellite view – view as seen from above or from a satellite

Sea – a body of salt water

Settlement – any form of human habitation, even a single dwelling, though usually applied to a group of dwellings

Snow – precipitation frozen into ice crystals that falls to earth in light white flakes

Sun – the star at the centre of our solar system around which Earth and seven other planets orbit

Surf – the foaming water produced by a powerful wave as it breaks on the rocks or the seashore

Tourism – the business of providing facilities and amenities for those travelling or staying in places for a relatively limited period of leisure time

Tropical – applying to the tropics, that is those areas of Earth that lie between latitude $23^030'N$ and $23^030'S$

Uluru – also known as Ayers Rock, a large sandstone rock formation in the southern part of Australia's Northern Territory

Village – a small group of houses and other buildings in a rural area

Waves – ridges of water resulting from the wind blowing over the surface of the sea

Your professional development

The writers of this publication subscribe to the process of 'curriculum making', a term used by the Geographical Association to describe *'what teachers do in their classrooms to personalise planning and tailor their teaching to pupils' needs'*. To continue this process you need to adopt and adapt this unit according to your pupils' needs and the principles set out on page 8. If you can engage in this process you will continue to travel significantly in terms of your own professional development.

This publication models the design for a 'prototype kit' for the study of a distant place with younger pupils, based on principles, and including activities which equip teachers to engage in 'curriculum-making' around other distant places:

- adopt the principle of balance of breadth and depth, keep a list of geography's 'big ideas' or concepts and vital skills in front of you and reflect on your pupils' prior learning and where you want to move them on to

- use your own and your colleagues' experiences of travel, internet map sites and images, globes and paper maps, travellers' and other websites, and good picture books and stories, select from your personal toolkit of activities and adapt, see 'geography explorers' (pages 10-11).

Further information
The GA's website has a range of resources available for members including a picture gallery offering free use of images www.geography.org.uk.

The *Primary Geography Handbook* (Scoffham, 2010) has a wealth of support and ideas. Available from *www.geography.org.uk/shop*.

Have you thought about receiving personal recognition for your work developing geography with your class? The GA's CPD courses offer accreditation. Check *www.geography.org.uk/cpdevents* for details and updates.

Have you thought about accreditation for your school? The Primary Geography Quality Mark is an evaluative tool that will help you assess how well your school is doing. You can apply for recognition at Bronze, Silver or Gold levels. See *www.geography. org.uk/cpdevents/qualitymarks*.

Join primary teachers on a professional forum to share ideas, queries and good practice *http://geographychampions.ning. com*.

Reference
Scoffham, S. (ed) (2010) *Primary Geography Handbook*. Sheffield: Geographical Association.

Subject coverage

	Little Blue Planet	Australia Here We Come!	Living in the Freezer	Neighbour-hood Watch!	Green Futures	Beside the Sea	Food for Thought	The UK
Suggested age range	Y1–3	Y1–3	Y2–4	Y3–5	Y3–5	Y4–6	Y4–6	Y4–6
Geographical enquiry	✔	✔	✔	✔	✔	✔	✔	✔
ICT	✔	✔	✔	✔	✔	✔	✔	✔
Global dimension	✔	✔	✔	◆	✔	◆	✔	◆
Sustainability and citizenship	✔	✔	✔	✔	✔	✔	✔	✔
Fieldwork	✔	✔	✔	✔	✔	✔	✔	✔
Map work	✔	✔	✔	✔	✔	✔	✔	✔
Range of places	✔	✔	✔	✔	✔	✔	✔	✔
Current issues	✔	✔	✔	✔	✔	✔	✔	✔
UK focus	◆			✔		✔	✔	✔
English	✔	✔	✔	✔	✔	✔	✔	✔
Mathematics	◆		✔		◆	◆		◆
Science	✔		✔		✔	✔	✔	
Creative arts	✔	✔	✔	✔	✔	✔		✔
History			✔	✔		◆	✔	✔
Design and technology						◆	◆	
Links to RE		◆	◆					◆

Key: ✔ more developed ◆ additional aspect